Natural Disasters

Droughts

by
Anne Ylvisaker

Consultant:
Joseph M. Moran, Ph.D.
Meteorologist
Education Program
American Meteorological Society

CAPSTONE
HIGH-INTEREST
BOOKS

an imprint of Capstone Press
Mankato, Minnesota

Capstone High-Interest Books are published by Capstone Press
151 Good Counsel Drive, P.O. Box 669, Mankato, Minnesota 56002
http://www.capstone-press.com

Library of Congress Cataloging-in-Publication Data
Ylvisaker, Anne.
    Droughts / by Anne Ylvisaker.
    p. cm.—(Natural disasters)
    Includes bibliographical references and index.
    Contents: Droughts—Why do droughts happen—The power of a drought—
Famous droughts—Surviving a drought.
    ISBN 0-7368-1505-8 (hardcover)
    1. Droughts—Juvenile literature. [1. Droughts.] I. Title. II. Natural disasters
(Capstone Press)
QC929.25 .Y59 2003
363.34'929—dc21   2002011448

Summary: Explains why droughts occur, describes the damage they inflict, the
difficulty in predicting them, and some of the worst droughts in history.

Editorial Credits
Chris Harbo and Roberta Schmidt, editors; Eric Kudalis, product planning editor;
    Patrick D. Dentinger, cover designer and illustrator; Jo Miller, photo researcher

Photo Credits
AP Photo/Timothy Jacobsen, 36
Bruce Coleman, Inc./John S. Flannery, 8; Wolfgang Bayer, 18; Jim Brandenburg, 20;
    Carol Hughes, 24; Gary Withey, 34; Norman Owen Tomalin, 41; Richard Walker, 44
Corbis/Reuters NewMedia Inc., 4; AFP, cover, 6; Bettmann, 26, 28
Corbis Sygma/Despotovic Dusko, 46
John Elk III, 15
NASA, 16
Photri-Microstock/Charles O. Cecil, 30, 32
Visuals Unlimited/Gary C. Will, 39

1 2 3 4 5 6 08 07 06 05 04 03

Table of Contents

Chapter 1

Droughts

In June 2001, the Chinese government ordered chemicals to be fired into the sky. The people waited. They hoped the chemicals would reach the clouds and make rain.

The spring had been unusually hot and dry. The summer was even hotter. By the end of June, temperatures reached over 100 degrees Fahrenheit (38 degrees Celsius), and no rain fell. Large cracks formed in the dry soil. Some land turned into desert. Wind picked up the soil and caused dust storms.

Many areas were affected by the drought, but northeastern China suffered the most. Some areas received less than half of their normal rainfall. Rivers, lakes, and reservoirs began to dry up. People and animals started to

Droughts can destroy farmland. Large cracks form in the dry soil. There is not enough moisture for the crops to grow.

A drought during the growing season hurts crops and leads to small harvests.

run out of water. Fish left the shallow streams and swam to deeper water. Cattle and sheep died because they could not find water to drink. Farmers' crops dried up and died. Some farmers had to leave their farms to search for work in cities.

More than 23 million people were affected by the drought in China. The months of hot, dry weather cost the country millions of dollars.

Droughts

Droughts happen when areas receive less rain than they need. Droughts are different from other natural disasters that come suddenly and end quickly. Droughts often begin slowly and can last weeks, months, or even years. Plants stop growing during a drought. Rivers, streams, and reservoirs dry up. People and animals sometimes do not have enough food to eat or water to drink. Droughts can lead to wildfires in fields and forests.

Droughts can take place anywhere in the world. North America, Europe, Africa, Asia, and Australia have suffered severe droughts. In poor countries, a drought can cause millions of people to starve and die. In wealthier countries, cities and towns sometimes run out of water.

Droughts are especially hard for farmers. A lack of rain during the growing season hurts crops and leads to small harvests.

Chapter 2

Why Droughts Happen

Droughts are caused by changes in the weather. Changes in Earth's water cycle, wind patterns, and air and water temperatures can cause drought conditions.

The Water Cycle

The water cycle moves water throughout the planet. Water travels from one place to another through evaporation, condensation, and precipitation.

The water cycle is the continual movement of water between Earth's oceans, land, and atmosphere. The oceans, the Sun, and the wind are the main parts of the water cycle. The Sun heats the oceans, lakes, soil, and plants to turn water into a vapor. Evaporation takes place

Changes in the Earth's water cycle can cause drought conditions.

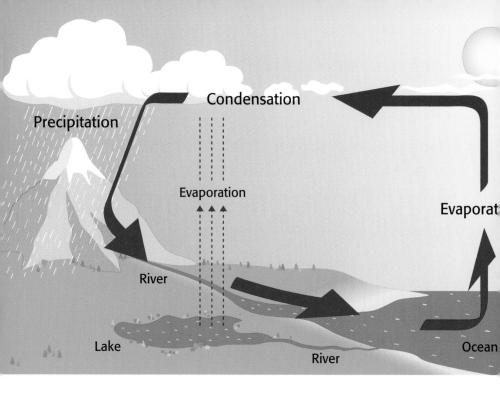

Condensation

Precipitation

Evaporation

Evaporat

River

Lake

Ocean

River

The water cycle moves water throughout the planet.

when water changes from a liquid to a vapor.

Within the atmosphere, some water vapor collects into tiny drops that create clouds. Condensation occurs when water vapor becomes a liquid. Wind moves clouds and water vapor over the land and sea.

Some clouds create rain, snow, or other forms of water. This water, called precipitation, falls from clouds to the Earth's surface.

10

Precipitation that reaches the ground may form rivers and streams. The water also may collect in lakes, ponds, and glaciers. Some water soaks into the ground. Rivers and streams drain back into the ocean. The water cycle then is complete.

During a drought, Earth's normal water cycle is interrupted. Water continues to evaporate from ocean and land surfaces, but fewer clouds form. The clouds that do form produce little or no precipitation.

Monsoons

Wind is an important part of Earth's water cycle. Seasonal winds, called monsoons, blow in one direction for part of the year. During the rest of the year, they blow in the other direction. In Asia, monsoons blow cool, dry air from north to south during fall and winter. In spring and summer, the monsoons change direction. Warm, moist air from the Indian Ocean travels from south to north. Asia's dry season is fall and winter. The wet season is spring and summer.

Low pressure systems usually create stormy weather.
High pressure systems usually create fair weather.

Wind cannot be controlled. Wet monsoons sometimes arrive later and end earlier than usual. The amount of rain that falls during a wet monsoon changes from year to year.

If the wet monsoon does not come, a drought affects the people who depend on the rain. The people of India and southeast Asia have suffered many droughts caused by failure of the wet monsoon.

Pressure Systems

In North America, periods of stormy weather are followed by periods of fair weather. High and low pressure systems create fair and stormy weather.

A low pressure system is a body of air that moves counter-clockwise as it travels across North America. Rising air within the low pressure system creates stormy weather. Air expands and cools as it rises. The cooler air causes water vapor to condense into clouds. Precipitation such as rain or snow falls.

A high pressure system is a body of air that moves clockwise as it travels across North America. Gently sinking air in the high pressure system creates fair weather. Air becomes denser as it warms and sinks. Clouds fail to form in a high pressure system. Without clouds, precipitation cannot fall.

Usually, low and high pressure systems follow one another across North America. The winds that steer these pressure systems might weaken. The pressure systems then stall.

When a high pressure system stays over one area for weeks or months, the weather stays fair and dry. A drought may develop.

During the summer of 1988, high pressure stayed over the central United States from May through early August. It caused one of the worst droughts in U.S. history.

Mountains

Mountains can affect the amount of rain and snow that falls. One side of a mountain can receive large amounts of rain while the other side receives very little. Wind pushes moist air upward into the atmosphere as it crosses over a mountain. As the air rises, it expands and cools, causing precipitation to fall. By the time the air reaches the other side of the mountain, little moisture remains. As the air continues down the mountain, it becomes denser, and the clouds evaporate. Very little precipitation falls on this side of the mountain.

The dry side of a mountain is called the rainshadow. The rainshadow may affect land

The side of a mountain that receives very little rain is called a rainshadow.

hundreds of miles beyond the base of the mountain. Deserts often form in a rainshadow.

El Niño and La Niña

In the tropical Pacific Ocean, temperatures change in the sea surface and in the air. These changes can cause droughts in other parts of the world.

Satellite images show temperature changes during El Niño.

El Niño is a period of unusually high temperatures over the central and eastern tropical Pacific Ocean. The warm ocean water heats the air and changes how the air moves. During El Niño, some areas of the world are much wetter than usual. Some areas are drier than usual. Southeast Asia and northern Australia have droughts during El Niño.

El Niño usually lasts from 12 to 18 months and happens about every 3 to 7 years.

La Niña is the opposite of El Niño. Sometimes it follows El Niño. During La Niña, sea surface temperatures are lower than usual in the central and eastern tropical Pacific Ocean. The cooler ocean water chills the air and changes how the air moves. During La Niña, some areas such as the Gulf Coast of the United States are drier than usual and may have a drought.

Chapter 3

The Power of a Drought

People and the environment suffer during a drought. Each year, cities struggle to save water. Farmers and ranchers watch crops fail and livestock die because of record high temperatures and little rain. Good farmland turns into desert-like land. In some parts of the world, droughts become so severe that people starve.

Effects on Agriculture

In the United States, droughts affect agriculture the most. Farmers depend on timely rainfall for their crops. A drought during the early stages of the growing season can ruin an entire crop.

During a drought, animals can die when they cannot find enough water.

A drought can ruin a farmer's entire crop.

Dry weather makes it difficult for seeds to sprout. Weeks of hot, dry weather make crops dry up and turn brown. If plants survive until harvest time, they usually are smaller and produce a smaller crop. Farmers then have little or no crop to sell.

Livestock also suffers during a drought. Plants in grazing lands dry up and die. Rivers, streams, and ponds dry up. Livestock then has less to eat and drink. Many farmers and ranchers must pump more water from the ground for their livestock. Crop losses and added costs for keeping livestock alive can drive farmers out of business. Farmers then may be forced off the farm and must find other jobs.

Droughts affect farmers in poor countries even more. Farmers in these countries often feed their families and livestock with the crops they grow. A severe drought can destroy their only source of food. Droughts often leave families and whole villages with no food to eat until the next growing season.

Effects on Society

In wealthy countries, droughts often cause problems, but few people die. When crops fail, most people buy food from other places. In cities suffering from a drought, people must save water. They may not be allowed to water their lawns. City government officials may ask citizens to use less water for baths and showers.

Deadly Droughts

Location	Years	Deaths
Sahel (Africa)	1984–1985	600,000
Sahel (Africa)	1972–1975	600,000
Russia	1932–1933	5 million
Russia	1921–1922	5 million
China	1920–1921	500,000
India	1899–1900	1 million
India	1896–1897	5 million
China	1892–1894	1 million
Russia	1891–1892	400,000
China	1876–1879	13 million
India	1876–1878	3.5 million
India	1865–1866	10 million

In rural areas, droughts can cause more serious problems. Wells for drinking water can dry up. People and animals in the country may be forced to leave their homes to find water.

In poor countries, severe droughts often lead to a shortage of food. This shortage, or famine, can lead to starvation. Famine strikes when crops fail and people cannot afford to buy food from other places.

Hunger is not the only danger for poor countries. During a severe drought, diseases kill more people than hunger. Sometimes, disease-causing organisms grow in well water and streams during a drought. People drink the water and become sick. Many people are forced to leave their homes to find food and clean water. Millions of people can die during severe droughts in poor countries.

Economic Impact

Droughts affect the price of food. Most people notice this effect at the supermarket. Fruits, vegetables, and other farm crops are

Rivers and ponds dry up during a drought.

in short supply during a drought. As the supply goes down, the price for these items goes up.

Droughts also affect a nation's businesses and industries. All businesses that depend on income from the use of water suffer during a drought. Transportation, energy, and tourism businesses are hurt the most. Water levels may become so low that boats and other watercraft cannot move easily in the water. Low water levels in rivers also reduce the amount of electricity generated by power plants. Tourists who enjoy fishing and other water sports may not visit an area during a drought. In 1988, a severe drought in the Midwest and Southeast cost the United States about $40 billion.

Environmental Impact

Droughts are hard on the environment. Long periods of hot, dry weather may cause small streams and ponds to completely dry up. Some animals die when they are unable to find water. Trees and brush in forests and prairies can quickly catch fire. Raging wildfires can burn up thousands of acres of land.

Long periods of dry weather and poor use of land can make the land like a desert. Farmland near a desert is especially fragile. Crops have shallow roots that do not hold the soil very well. Some farmers plant crops every year without giving the soil a rest. This practice can cause soil to dry out. If a drought follows, farmland near a desert can become part of the desert.

Chapter 4

Famous Droughts

Throughout history, droughts have affected people and the environment. People study droughts from the past to learn how to deal with future droughts.

The Dust Bowl

In the late 1800s and early 1900s, thousands of people moved to the plains of the United States to plant crops in the rich soil. Midwestern states such as Kansas, Oklahoma, and Nebraska had large prairies. Settlers plowed up the grass and planted large fields of wheat. For many years, farmers harvested large yields from the rich soil. As the demand for wheat worldwide increased, farmers plowed more fields.

Large dust storms swept across the midwestern United States in the 1930s.

Wheat has shorter roots than prairie grass. The short roots did not hold the soil in place as well as the prairie grass did. In 1931, a pattern of dry weather and high winds settled into the middle of the United States. Wheat fields could not hold down the soil. Large dust storms swept across the Midwest. Oklahoma, Texas, Kansas, and Colorado suffered the worst damage. Within a few years, productive farmland was turned into a dusty landscape called the Dust Bowl.

A severe drought gripped the middle of the country from 1931 to 1937. From Texas to Canada, rich farmland turned into fields of dust. The soil dried up and blew away in dust storms that turned the sky black. People got sick from breathing so much dirt. Grasshoppers swarmed farms, eating what remained of the crops. Thousands of families abandoned their farms and moved to California. The whole country suffered because farms were not producing crops for food.

During the 1930s, thousands of families left the Midwest and moved to Oregon and California.

The Sahel

The Sahel is a wide band of grassy land that runs the width of North Africa. The Sahel lies just south of the Sahara Desert and north of the African rainforest. It includes parts of 10 countries. It is home to more than 100 million people.

The Sahel has a monsoon climate. The rainy season is spring and summer. The dry season is fall and winter. Droughts are common in the Sahel. They often last many years. Since the late 1960s, the Sahel has been struck by several droughts.

The first major drought during this time period caused widespread crop failure. Many people tried to plant crops again the next season, but rainfall still did not come. Without a crop for food, people ate the seeds they needed to plant the following season. Cattle and other livestock started to die. With each passing season, less food and water were available. Famine began to take over the Sahel.

Droughts are common in the Sahel of North Africa.

Some people in the Sahel travel long distances to find water during a drought.

The drought continued for several years. Families moved from place to place to find food and water. People grew weak. Their bodies could not fight off disease. From 1972 to 1975, more than 600,000 people died of starvation and disease in the Sahel.

When the drought ended, farmers planted more crops than ever. They planted grain every year. But the soil was poor. It needed a year to rest between crops. Farmers could not afford to lose a year of planting. The next drought struck in the mid-1980s. Crops failed quickly in the poor soil. Once again, hundreds of thousands of people died of starvation and disease in the Sahel.

Midwestern United States, 1987–1989

The most expensive natural disaster in U.S. history was the 1987–1989 drought. The total economic cost of the drought was almost $40 billion. People in 35 states suffered from the 3-year drought.

The northern part of the Great Plains was hardest hit by the drought. Rainfall totals were 50 to 80 percent below normal in the Great Plains and Northwest in 1988. Farmers in North Dakota, South Dakota, and Minnesota watched their corn and soybean crops dry up and die.

In 1988, the drought created dry conditions that led to wildfires in Yellowstone National Park in Wyoming. Lightning strikes started

large forest fires that burned almost 800,000 acres (323,760 hectares) of land. More than 9,000 firefighters fought the blazes. The cost to control the fires reached $120 million.

The Mississippi River's water levels fell during the drought. Areas of the river became narrow. River barges carrying coal and grain had to move slowly up and down the river. In December 1988, part of the Mississippi River was closed for two days because of the low water levels. Shipping delays caused many companies to lose millions of dollars.

During a drought, crops do not get enough water. They dry up, turn brown, and die.

Chapter 5

Surviving a Drought

Droughts continue to happen throughout the world. Meteorologists study past weather patterns to learn more about why droughts happen and when they can be expected. People then may have time to prepare for droughts. Good planning can reduce the effects of droughts.

Predicting Droughts

Droughts are difficult to predict. People do not always know if dry weather will lead to a drought. Droughts begin slowly and gradually become more severe.

Meteorologists study weather patterns year-round. They collect information about areas that receive little rain over weeks and

Good planning can reduce the effects of a drought. ⟵

months. Meteorologists warn people when the conditions are right for a drought.

Some scientists study tree rings to learn about droughts. Each year, a tree grows a new layer of wood around it. These layers create rings. When a tree gets enough water, it grows a thick layer of wood. During a drought, the tree grows a thin ring. Scientists can study tree rings to learn how often droughts have happened. They look for patterns in the tree rings to help predict when an area might expect another drought.

Planning for Droughts

Scientists have studied droughts like the ones in the Sahel and the Midwestern United States. They understand the mistakes people made in the years before the drought. Farmers now learn how to use the land more wisely. They plant trees to keep crops shaded. They plant lines of trees close together to create windbreaks. The windbreaks help to protect plants and soil from strong winds. Farmers

Windbreaks help to protect plants and soil from strong winds.

also plant their crops in different patterns to help keep water from draining off the fields.

Cities also try to prepare for droughts. Many towns make emergency plans. These plans tell city leaders how much water the town should save in case of a drought. Emergency plans also provide rules for using water when dry weather reduces the water supply.

Clean water is a limited resource. People can help save water to prepare for a drought. They can collect rainwater from rain gutters and use it to water plants. They can also plant trees and shrubs that need little water to live. Indoors, people can save water by taking shorter showers and turning off faucets while brushing their teeth. People can also save water by fixing leaky faucets.

Droughts can be some of the most harmful natural disasters on Earth. They often begin slowly and last for weeks, months, or even years. Droughts are difficult to predict and cannot be prevented. But people can prepare for them by using water wisely.

⟶ **Clean water is a limited resouce. People should use water wisely.**

Words To Know

condensation (kon-den-SAY-shuhn)—the change of water from a gas to a liquid

evaporation (e-vap-uh-RAY-shuhn)—the change of water from a liquid to a gas

famine (FAM-uhn)—serious shortage of food resulting in widespread hunger and death

monsoon (mon-SOON)—a very strong seasonal wind that brings heavy rains or hot, dry weather

organism (OR-guh-niz-uhm)—a living plant or animal; bacteria are microorganisms that can cause disease.

precipitation (pri-sip-i-TAY-shuhn)—water that falls from clouds to the Earth's surface; precipitation can be rain, hail, sleet, or snow.

reservoir (REZ-ur-vwar)—a natural or artificial structure that is a holding area for a large amount of water

To Learn More

Bender, Lionel. *Heat and Drought.* Living with the Weather. Austin, Tex.: Raintree Steck-Vaughn, 1998.

Bundey, Nikki. *Drought and People.* The Science of Weather. Minneapolis: Carolrhoda Books, 2001.

Chambers, Catherine. *Drought.* Wild Weather. Chicago: Heinemann Library, 2002.

Coombs, Karen Mueller. *Children of the Dust Days.* Picture the American Past. Minneapolis: Carolrhoda Books, 2000.

Newson, Lesley. *Devastation!: The World's Worst Natural Disasters.* New York: DK Publishing, 1998.

Useful Addresses

American Refugee Committee
430 Oak Grove Street
Suite 204
Minneapolis, MN 55403

Drought Monitor
National Drought Mitigation Center
P.O. Box 830749
Lincoln, NE 68583-0749

Federal Emergency Management Agency
500 C Street SW
Washington, DC 20472

Water Education Foundation
717 K Street
Suite 317
Sacramento, CA 95814

Internet Sites

Do you want to learn more about Droughts?
Visit the FACT HOUND at *http://www.facthound.com*

FACT HOUND can track down many sites to help you.
All the FACT HOUND sites are hand-selected by Capstone
Press editors. FACT HOUND will fetch the best, most accurate
information to answer your questions.

IT IS EASY! IT IS FUN!
1) Go to *http://www.facthound.com*
2) Type in: 0736815058
3) Click on "FETCH IT" and FACT HOUND will put you on
the trail of several helpful links.

**You can also search by subject or book title. So, relax
and let our pal FACT HOUND do the research for you!**

Index